Daily Inspirations For Your Spirit, Soul And Body

VIKKI KENNEDY JOHNSON

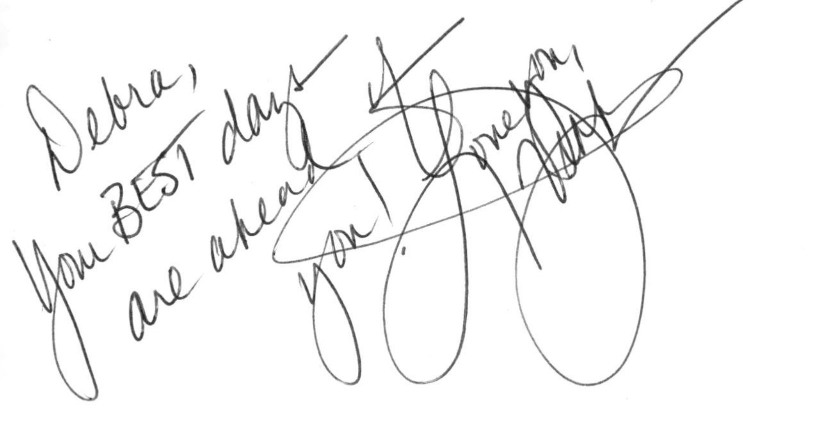

VIKKI-ISMS
Vikki Kennedy-Johnson

Published by Pecan Tree Publishing, February 2013
Hollywood, Fl
www.pecantreebooks.com

Library of Congress Control Number: 2013901001

ISBN: 978-0-9888969-2-5

PECAN TREE PUBLISHING
Hollywood, Fl.
www.pecantreepress.com

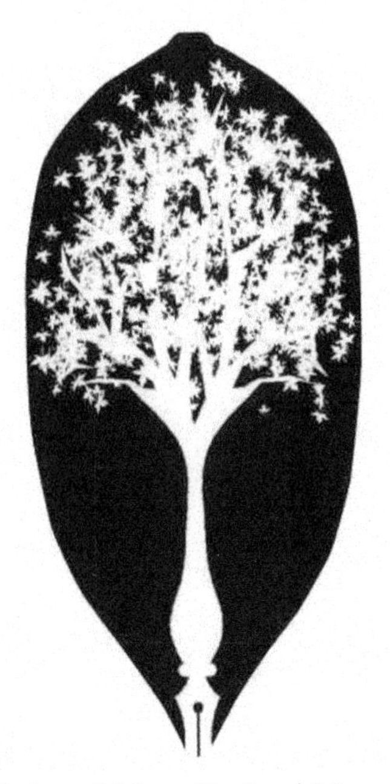

New Voices | New Styles | New Vision

Here is what other people are saying about Vikki Johnson.....

Thoughtful, powerful and passionate are words that come to mind when I think of Vikki Johnson. A connector and facilitator of dreams who carefully and thoughtfully does whatever she can to impart life, love and hope freely into the hearts and minds of the people she encounters. Discerning and decisive about her space, she flows in her power in a very confident, yet, grounded way that compels her audiences near and far to reach higher and dig deeper for the greater more victorious part of themselves. Her passion for people, life and love is awesome, genuine and influential. To relate to her or simply be in her presence is to be stretched and challenged to live on the edge by faith. In no uncertain terms, Vikki shares her heart and her truth without denying the desires and dignity of her listener. In her own special way, she challenges people to search and find answers that already sit within. My life is better because of her friendship. A sea of fabulous women and men alike are much closer to their purpose and destiny because she intentionally operates in her own.

Veronica Very, Founder, Very Bright Foundation

Vikki Kennedy Johnson is a dynamic, thought-provoking speaker, visionary and empowerment strategist. She is dedicated to living a life of authenticity with a carefree spirit of peace, while shaking up the world with the power of truth. She generously contributes services and resources to those underserved and is a gift to community stakeholders. Vikki has clearly made a positive impact in the lives of women and girls alike through her outreached hands and heart. Vikki Kennedy Johnson is incredibly kind and a wise woman who truly "walks the talk" making us all much better with each step she takes.

Carolyn White Washington, Executive Director, Sisters4Sisters, Inc

Vikki Johnson is one of the most captivating personalities and brilliant minds our modern world has the privilege of experiencing. Her insightful and "box-free" teachings make a lasting impact in the lives of her audiences worldwide. Vikki has never met a stranger and has a unique way of drawing people in. Whether experiencing her books, broadcasts, workshops or seminars, people gain the tools and strategies necessary to not only overcome and survive, but to triumph and thrive in life.

Elder Veda McCoy, Educator, Scholar, and Founder of LifePower

Vikki Kennedy-Johnson has a charismatic, wise and giving spirit. Always willing to share her gifts with others she has even been brave and self-less enough to donate an organ to a family member. There are very few women like Vikki, who are open to sharing lessons learned over the years both professionally and spiritually. The first day I met her, she suggested a book for me that changed the course of my life. Though I have been working in my career for 20-years, I have never had a mentor. Even though we hadn't known each other very long, I sensed in Vikki, the exact qualities I desired in a mentor and asked her if she would consider becoming mine. She immediately agreed and has generously shared valuable advice and insight with me ever since.

Wendi Cherry, Music Industry Professional

Vikki is a woman of distinction, full of life, wisdom, energy, and determination to win. She deposits gems into the lives off all she comes in contact with. I see her as a mentor extraordinaire, a faithful and true friend, a woman of immense inner beauty, power and strength, and a woman passionate about all that God calls her to. She truly is "Every Woman" chosen by God to set the captives free!

Leslie Atley, Business Associate

I love Vikki Johnson!! Upon hearing her deliver a heart-felt invocation almost ten years ago at the NABFEME (National Association of Female Executives in Music and Entertainment), I knew at that moment that Vikki had to be in my life - then and always.

Vikki joined my husband and me in marriage in 2003; since then she has held our hands through the challenges and joys of marriage, the birth of our daughter, career transitions and real life matters. She has always offered hope and a timely prayer for us to hold strong - no matter what comes. Vikki Johnson is authentic and a gift to all she encounters.

-Karen Taylor Bass, The PR Expert and Founder of The 'Brand' New Mommy

"Her life is a tribute to GREAT as she looks to inspire, exalt, and empower -

She's the type of lady that should be pampered daily, hour after hour; because she puts in the work, not just with her hands, but with her mind.-

I said it before, and I'll say it again, she's a True Queen, True Leader and Hard Find!"

- Raymond Pretlor, Entrepreneur and Spoken Word Artist

Vikki is more than an inspiring woman of God she is a source of encouragement and love. Her words are filled with wisdom and wise instruction. She is a woman that I know I can call when I myself need clarity. She always has the right divinely-inspired words to help me see things from a Godly perspective. She is a sister, mentor, and friend. She is one of God's finest teachers and motivators. She is also one of the many blessings I have been given in life. I absolutely LOVE her!

Dani LoveStrong, Founder of Strong Lovers Online Community, Blogger, and Social Media Strategist

Vikki is a great friend who took an interest in my life wanting only the best for me and my family. She encourages me to achieve, be successful, focused and asked for nothing in return. Life has taught me to appreciate this woman in more ways than I could ever have space to express. I gain energy from her words. Without ever looking into my eyes filled with pain she gave me encouragement that kept me focused on God. She told me it would hurt but not always. She guided me back to the light that led me to the One that had the answers, God. As I read a book she suggested, I learned that I could gain my hind feet and walk up the mountain. As I continued to heal she continued to direct me to the vision for my life, she lead me to speak victory and to believe in myself. I saw the vision clearly in my life. However, without her little notes and special comments just when I needed them, I wouldn't be walking in total victory today. I thank God for her daily. I was talking to my husband and told him, Vikki has done more for me than people I see every day. God is good and I thank Him for the person of Vikki Kennedy Johnson. Because of Vikki I can stand and teach women today as she did for me. For me, Vikki means victory.

Karen McKoy, Happy Wife, Proud Mom, Grandmother, Vice President of Spiritual Life and Women's Ministry Teacher, U.S. Military

Vikki Johnson is a professional and spiritual leader with over 20 years of experience inspiring, motivating and uplifting everyone that crosses her path. As a mentor to countless young people, Vikki is always willing to lend an ear and give thoughtful advice. As my colleague in the Corporate Social Responsibility sector, she is dependable, thorough and passionate about uplifting the community. I can always rely on Vikki whenever I need her and count her as one of my closest friends. Always looking to learn and grow, Vikki has done countless training and development programs making her a master teacher, counselor and adviser to all that cross her path. Genuine, kind and honest, Vikki has so much to share with the world and I highly recommend this book for anyone that is on a quest for enlightenment and peace.

Nneka A. Norville, Corporate Social Responsibility Strategist

Poised, confident, God-fearing and real, Vikki Johnson is truly every woman. A woman who wears many hats but who does so with grace and class leaving many wondering how she does it and still come out on top. She's God-assured, aware of who she is and she understands the importance of balance and living a God-inspired life. Her down-to-earth nature causes all who meet her to instantly feel welcomed and accepted. Her courage to speak the truth in love is inspiring and her tell-it-like-it-is attitude invokes freedom and encourages women to embrace their God given destiny and live their best life now - in the most extraordinary way. Her message is simple yet powerful and because of this, she's a woman to watch and learn from. Sometimes challenging with the goal to provoke change, her words will take you from 'ouch' to 'empowered' simultaneously. It's the gift from God that makes her great, that makes her relatable and that makes her unique. She's the sister everyone should have and the friend everyone deserves. Vikki Johnson is every woman!

Rokia Ballard, Mentee

Dedications

I dedicate this work to the women who gave me their very best example of LOVE while they were here on earth as humans "disguised" as Angels. I miss each of you dearly and am grateful that your love still guides me as I show love to others through the words of wisdom in this book.

Elizabeth Williams
Marion E. Kennedy
Dr. Geraldine McInnis

Table of Contents

Acknowledgements

To my Mini Me who is now writing her own "isms". I love you and you will always be my little girl and a reflection of God's love for me.

To my family, friends, and teachers/mentors of life, love, and the pursuit of service whom I adore - THANK YOU for being an amazing village of support. You know who you are because I show you, tell you, and make sure you know how much you mean to me as often as I can.

To my amazing, loving, and kindhearted GENTLE MAN - thank you for looking for me and finding me when you did. Living a purpose-filled life is even more fun when you have someone to share it with the way I'm blessed to share it with you.

To those of you who read my Vikki-isms daily, listen to my weekly radio feature, have read my other books, allowed me to counsel you, perform your wedding, eulogize a loved one, or simply have been encourage by my journey in one way or another - YOU inspire me to grow and keep going daily.

To E. Claudette Freeman and Pecan Tree Publishing - I am so grateful, humbled, and honored that God allowed me to find you in the place of my beginning. I am SO excited for you and all that God is manifesting in your life. Thank you for encouraging me to "get up and get back to writing!" Thank you for pushing me to birth what was inside me in finished book form. Just thank you from the center of my heart. You are not just my editor, cheerleader, trainer, coach, and voice of reason, but my sister and my friend.

Foreword

From the window of my dining room I peer out into what is unmistakably paradise. Mesmerized, as the tropical palm trees whisper sweet nothings to the warm winds and the sun kisses the coconuts like longtime lovers and friends, I am overtaken with a message in my heart: *Only THIS is real.* And by *THIS,* she means love...unconditional love.

But before getting swept up into this blissful moment with Mother Nature, my mind is interrupted with the idea that even though *THIS* realness is what we all desire - this unspeakable sense of inner joy, harmony and serenity - many of us may never attain it. And when we do, it is often in fleeting moments that are simply shortened by the fear interjected from our own sneaky inner saboteur.

Quick to arm myself with a brighter and broader side, I ask: What do we need to make and sustain these fundamental shifts...changes for the better? What do we need to trust the process of the journey of the soul? What do we need to LIVE loved...like THIS?

Frankly, I'm not sure if it is the tens of thousands of hours as a psychiatrist journeying with people through their darkest hours or digging folks out of emotional and physical hoards on *A& E's Emmy-nominated cable television show Hoarders.* But I'm reminded that what we humans need is INSPIRED soul connection. We need to know that we are not alone in the world. That we are loved. We long to know that someone's in our corner cheering us on. Someone who understands us. Someone who has just the right thing to say at just the right moment. I can't help but to wonder if it's encoded in our DNA.

Carl Jung, the father of modern psychiatry is known to have said "Nobody, as long as he moves about among the chaotic currents of life, is without trouble." I believe this to be true. By no means am I pessimistic or trouble seeking. But at some pivotal times in my life these simple words have served as a powerful reminder that perfection is not the goal. The goal is simply progression. *What an incredible gift!*

Over the course of history we have been blessed with individuals who bestow us with these life course altering reminders. These individuals are those to whom God gave a special gift - the ability to use the power of prose to inspire, encourage and sometimes even provoke us to give life our very best shot. Seeming almost effortlessly, quotes of these greats even in their absence continue to charge us with searching our hearts and minds for higher truths and actualizing our highest emotional potential. Their words pour out life energizing force in ways that timelessly defy the human mind.

Without a doubt Vikki Kennedy Johnson has been gifted with this great and sacred ability. I'm simply honored to stand witness in real-time as the healing pierce of her poetic and wise words consciously shifts humankind. Because it has and it will.

Vikki-isms is an invaluable treasure trove of these pearls of wisdom, a collection of universal truths interwoven in a way that meets you right where you are, leaving you feeling that your prayers for connection have been heard...and answered.

I imagine this volume of gems finding a home in your purse, on your coffee table or on your night stand, somewhere close by ready for you to crack it open at just those right times. And as a healer, my secret hope is that when you catch yourself caught up in old patterns that aren't serving anymore, falling into behaviors that aren't loving, but block you from living a life filled with joy and vitality that you will let Vikki-isms be your friendly pocket spiritual guide. My hope is that you will let the divine spark in your heart be reignited. My prayer is that you will be reminded in those moments when YOU need it most: *Only THIS is real.*

Melva Green, MD, MBA, MPH
Psychiatrist/Expert on A&E's Hoarders

Introduction

I'm back and ready to love on you with a passionate and heartfelt **"WOW!"** - After waking up in the hospital recovery room after giving my cousin a kidney almost two years ago, God told me that He was going to **WOW** me every day for the rest of my life. He said that I was to squeeze every ounce of joy, laughter, love, and light out of every moment of every day from that point forward.

That is what this book is all about. Vikki-isms is a collection of my "wordsmith" tendencies, my emotional recollections, spiritual revelations, and intellectual reckonings of awakening, expanded consciousness, and the realization that the only thing that truly matters in this life is how much love we get to experience. **WOW!**

I'm so happy and grateful that the gift of writing that God has given me reaches, touches, and heals others. That is who I am - a Healer. **WOW!** I always knew that the call on my life to help others was greater than any mistake I had ever made. I have come to accept that everything I've been through was for me to grow through to reach back and help someone else.

Several years ago God sent a wonderful woman into my life who gave me unconditional love and acceptance. She was an amazing spirit who impacted me in ways I often did not understand. We had an incredible bond that we rarely discussed but knew existed. I mean we would finish each other's sentences, call each other when we were thinking about each other at the same time, laugh together and cry together. She was an early adopter of social media - specifically Facebook. She loved people and daily logged on to bless with her writings what had quickly become her growing Facebook family. She was affectionately known as "Dr. Mom". I vividly remember the last conversation we had before she unexpectedly and suddenly passed away. It too was full of laughter. Shortly thereafter I had a dream in which she told me to pick up her mantle on Facebook and continue what she had started." This is my first time sharing this publicly and it is significant because I had no desire at all to even have a Facebook page. This book is the result of me accepting that torch and running with it. She has done it again - blessed my life with her gentle nudge of love. **WOW!**

So as Dr. Mom would so often say, "Beloved, I celebrate your life today!" Now turn the page, be Inspired, be Incouraged, be Incredible, be Inpowered to uncover your own journey of WOW! (By the way **WOW** simply stands for: **W**ords **o**f **W**isdom.)

Vikki-isms

Daily Inspirations For Your Spirit, Soul And Body

Chapter 1

Love, the way God intended, will bring you PEACE; not leave you in PIECES! Even still - know that what you have left is enough to love and be loved.

Don't be fooled! 99.9% of the time, the grass ain't greener on the other side; it's just spray painted; or the water bill is a LOT higher! I'm telling you it's a trick! Water your OWN doggone grass!

Dear God, Thank You for showing me the love You created me to experience before I started helping You!

As I Ponder...

I love you does not mean I have to endure the consequences of your unhealthy decisions! Note to self: I LOVE ME MORE!

When your misery becomes greater than your fear of change, you'll start making different decisions. My dear Beloved - DO IT (whatever it is) AFRAID. That's courage!

Rejoice! It had to be ruined in order to be restored! Now you have room for what you should have had in the first place!

What Stirs in My Spirit Is ...

A woman is natural INspiration! Our INfluence lies IN our ability to tap INto our INnocence, INtegrity, INtuition, INtentions, INtimacy, INtelligence and INdividuality! Notice IN-ne-thing? It's an INside job ladies! (Inspired by a message from C. Sterling Davis)

Please STOP using your past pain as an excuse for your current craziness! Everyone has survived something. Further, it didn't come to kill you - it came to make you stronger! Enough already! With love - GOD!

THIS (whatever it is you are going through) and THAT (whatever it is you have been through already) had to happen to qualify you for the HOW DO YOU LIKE ME NOW blessing that is on the way! Oh it's coming, so give thanks for it now!

As I Reflect ...

If you're going to pack, print a boarding pass, go through security, and find your gate - GET ON THE DOGGONE PLANE!

In the tense political climate of 2011, I observed that the Tea Party is just LOUD - not LARGE! The message to you: Don't mistake the voices of a few as the voice of the majority! Now get up and fight! The greater One is in you!

At this very moment, what you no longer have is irrelevant. What you have left is ENOUGH for you to be restored!

As I Ponder...

Square your shoulders, hold your head high, smile and get yourself together! REJECTION IS GOD'S PROTECTION HONEY BEAR! Keep it cute and keep it moving! God's BEST for you is just ahead! To experience fulfillment, live, love, and laugh today like it's your last chance; and then tomorrow - DO IT AGAIN!

Early one morning, I received a phone call telling me that a dear friend was killed in a terrible accident! I'm sure I told her I loved her the last time we talked! Then as I began to mourn, she called to tell me she was okay. The person killed was someone with the same name! I exhaled. Tell the people you love that you love them every chance you get.

What Stirs in My Spirit Is ...

Don't adjust your efforts to THEIR opinions! Who are THEY anyway? Strengthen what you have left and succeed in spite of THEM! I'm just saying...

Just like when you turn on the light darkness dissipates; when you turn on LOVE fear disappears! FLIP THE SWITCH!

We were created for freedom; which is an intrinsic or internal state of BEing! Bondage is unnatural! You won't experience liberated living until your desire to be free is GREATER than your desire to only feel good! You must be willing to risk losing it all to have it all!

As I Reflect ...

Pure joy to me is Mojo singing, being on the beach, chocolate cake, and seeing something crazy like CNN's Wolf Blitzer doing the dougie w/ Doug E. Fresh at the Soul Train Awards. (It was SO funny!)

The truth is many of us can't run to love because we don't know what love is! For example, familiarity is NOT love! Just because you are used to it does not mean you have to live with it. Let's work on this definition of LOVE! Love is...

I'm sitting on a plane right now and I hear so clearly - tell them to RETURN TO LOVE! You were not created to live in fear! You are loveable and therefore able TO LOVE! Run to it, embrace it, and experience the relief you've been longing for!

As I Ponder...

Stop punishing people for loving you! You get back the same energy you give. Face your fears and unlock your heart so you can stop the pain! LOVE is waiting to heal you!

MY SISTER YOU ARE RESILIENT! I don't care what has happened in your life it's not who you are! It has only added to your value and your voice. GIRLS ROCK and WE ARE RESILIENT!

Where you are is not all there is! God has a plan for your life and a purpose for your pain. So whether you run, walk, crawl, or need to be carried for awhile - KEEP MOVING forward! It gets better - that's a promise!

What Stirs in My Spirit Is ...

Truth comes in all forms! We need to WAKE UP, get involved, PAY ATTENTION, and not just be a hearer of the word but DO SOMETHING in and for our communities!

I'm here to tell you there is nothing like sharing your WHOLENESS with another WHOLE PERSON and not settling for a piece of a person's brokenness to go with your broken self'! Gather your broken pieces FIRST so you can get ready for love!

It's romantic to say you feel complete when your special other has entered your life. Yet, the purpose of relationship is not to have another who might complete you, but to have another with whom you might share your completeness.

As I Reflect ...

Chapter 2

Rejection doesn't mean stop - it means NEXT! Up ahead there's something BETTER; so keep moving. When you get THERE you'll thank God for blocking THAT! (Laughing and loving my life!)

Acceptance is the bridge to authenticity! Your capacity to love someone else is based on your capacity TO LOVE ALL OF YOUR TRUE SELF! Today's exercise is ACCEPTANCE - please join me in accepting self.

The essence of a woman's beauty exudes from the inside and flows outward! That's a given! So today's exercise in BEING a powerful Goddess is to declare 3 physical attributes that you love about yourself - GO....

As I Ponder...

A woman has the capacity to love a man so richly that he feels like Superman EVERYDAY! My name is Lois Lane! LOL! Describe and speak your power even if you don't know who your Superman is yet!

I see myself in the future and things look so much better! What do you see? Say it - believe it - expect it. IT - IS COMING...SOON!

Believe it or not, Hip Hop artist DJ Khaled in his hit All We Do is Win, came straight from Exodus 17! God told Moses in Exodus 17... As long as your hands are raised you'll prevail! Keep your hands up people! ALL WE DO IS WIN WIN WIN NO MATTER WHAT!

What Stirs in My Spirit Is ...

You will no longer be allowed to soak up my energy if you're not going to BE BETTER and turn it into power to help someone else! EXCUSES ARE WACK!

You are not finished when you lose, you're finished when you quit! Keep it cute and keep it moving!

I'm not afraid to ask for what I want and you shouldn't be either! The love you give is the love coming back to you! Thank you for loving self!

As I Reflect ...

Replay: When it mattered, they didn't care and now that they care, it DOES NOT matter! I'm not angry, I'm just freeeee and it feels good!

The purpose of (womb) man or woman is o receive the invisible from a man and make it visible. Wow! (Inspired by C. Sterling Davis)

Men want peace not just that piece (and by the way, they will take that piece if you offer it). Men want stimulating conversation not complaints, internal balance not just external beauty, support not selfishness! Please STOP acting like his mother! Now work your femininity and your bliss will follow!

As I Ponder...

There is power, power wonder working power in the heel of a shoe. There is power, power, wonder working power in the precious heel of a shoe! Ladies I'm telling you - HEELS HAVE POWER! Kick some things and people with your power; just trying to help!

Ladies, wrap your LOVE around YOUR man so phenomenally, that if he is ever trapped somewhere without you - IN HIS MIND - he'll be free because you've given him a taste of heaven on earth!

Choose to live in the light with your truth and not in the dark with your lies! TRUTH ALWAYS WINS in a beautiful way!

What Stirs in My Spirit Is ...

Just live in the light with your truth and not in the dark with your lies! Truth always wins!

We deserve to be a person's CHOICE in the midst of their wholeness, not just a pacifier in the midst of their brokenness! (Clarity is priceless!).

I recently discovered that neuroplasticity of the brain helps the brain recover after trauma! Then, my next thought was - WOW - God has given us everything we need to bounce back. It is our response-ability to KEEP MOVING FORWARD; again - because you CAN!

As I Reflect ...

You are stuck because you CHOOSE not to move! Here's a thought - ASK FOR HELP! So much LOVE is waiting to heal you! YOU CAN DO THIS!

Healing comes with accepting yourself JUST the way you are and having the courage to love yourself enough to grow from where you are! BE healed so you can BE happy!

Peace is an internal state of being that is reflected in your external reality! Chaos externally is a CREDIBLE WITNESS that there is chaos internally!

As I Ponder...

Intrinsically men want a woman who understands the Power of P - mmmmm - I'm talking about PEACE (laughing). If you understand this P the others will come naturally! Be easy, it's ALL good and it's all God!

Everything God did was so we could RELATE to Him in the most intimate way! Your man is like God; if you praise him, he will bless you, he will reveal mysteries to you, and he will let you into the deepest places in his heart and WOW you! GIRL PRAISE YOUR MAN! Amen? Amen!

If you are difficult to deal with here's a tip: When you have to come back across that bridge (and you will), just know it won't be there because YOU BURNED IT DOWN! (Inspired after days of dealing with egos, bad attitudes, and arrogance)

What Stirs in My Spirit Is ...

God put Adam and Eve in the Garden of Eden Naked - not with clothes on! You're most free when you're not hiding what should be exposed!

The more you tell him how WONDERFUL he is - the more he will fill your world with WONDER (that which arouses awe, admiration, and amazing orgasms)! YES I SAID IT!

You will bring out the LEADER in your man if you will FOLLOW him! I hear you screaming - WHAT? But the payoff is this; he'll begin to feel like a KING, build a kingdom around you and treat you like a QUEEN!

As I Reflect ...

If your man wants to meet you somewhere and it's raining, don't complain! Get your umbrella and GO! There's always another woman who doesn't mind getting wet!

Rick Warren said: "How you look can attract a man's eye, but what connects his heart is how you make him FEEL when you talk to him!" Read this over and over 'til you get it!

Live in surrender to your OPTIONS, not chained as a prisoner to your obstacles! There's ALWAYS another way! ALWAYS...

Love is in need of love today and it is the ONLY thing that matters! Love comforts, love covers, love cares, love caresses, love creates a confluence of MORE LOVE! I love you LOVE! Pass it on!

As I Ponder...

After all the things I've been through, I'm STILL standing!

Patterns don't lie...PAY ATTENTION! It's either reaaaaaaaaaal good or retarded! (Now that is funny! And that is true!)

Friendship is most valuable when no words are necessary! (Inspired by Dr. Horace Smith)

What Stirs in My Spirit Is ...

Movement creates opportunity! Do something and what's next will appear!

If you are m-i-s-e-r-a-b-l-e that is your CHOICE! Begin to tell your story the way you want it to be and your life will follow! You have what you say. Now go re-create what you don't like!

When it mattered they didn't care. Now that they care, it REALLY doesn't matter! Thank them for teaching you how resilient you are!

As I Reflect ...

Chapter 3

Harold Melvin and Blue Notes sang it best: "FEELS so good loving somebody and somebody loves you back - that's a fact!" Now imagine the feeling. Feel the feeling, BE the feeling. VOILA! Love manifested!

Same ole thing, same ole issues, same ole frustration - HELLO - same ole YOU! Do something different Darling...it really works!

If you have to perform to feel it, then it is NOT love! You are perfectly loveable right now. (You're welcome) LOVE YOU!

As I Ponder...

You have to surrender to freedom and fun to enjoy it! It's not THAT serious. Lighten up - LAUGH, LOVE, and LIVE!

What you call work is really RELATIONSHIP! Do it from a place of love and watch it transform before your eyes!

Their lack of planning is NOT your emergency! Keep it easy like Sunday morning! I'm just saying...

What Stirs in My Spirit Is ...

I can see clearly now the PAIN is gone! It's gonna be a bright, bright, Son shiny day!

Depression is suppression of pain that needs to be released through expression! Get it out and get your life back! Therapy is NOT a bad word!

Release the fear that surrounds your PERFECT self and you will access your power. Remember LOVE was here first; so allow what ALREADY is and live!

As I Reflect ...

WHY NOT?!

The tragedy of not being true to self is that you often get stuck doing permanent things with temporary people that teach you permanent lessons! Now that one was good to me (LOL)

FAVOR rarely makes sense to those looking in from the outside! SO STOP TRYING TO EXPLAIN it and just enjoy it!

As I Ponder...

God uses the foolish things of the world to confound the wise and the RELIGIOUS!

Don't you worry one bit; your sacrifice (which most people don't understand), was simply a setup for a season of miracles in your life! EXHALE...

Relationship is NOT about who has the power. It's about serving one another! Different huh? It's a beautiful thing once you master it!

What Stirs in My Spirit Is ...

Environment is an internal experience not an external reality! (Neal Donald Walsch). Consequently, the atmosphere MUST change when you show up in all your loveliness!

Ladies don't be a penny out here looking for a quarter! BE the person you want to find! Simply put...give a man a PEACEFUL place to rest and he'll gladly succumb to your feminine pulchritude! LISTEN, LEARN, and LOVE!

If it's not perfect then it doesn't matter to my MOMENT at that moment!

As I Reflect ...

It's really NOT as complicated as you're making it. Live in the ease of God!

You're not living authentically until WHO you are and WHAT you do align!

When you're grateful for what you have then what you want shows up to be appreciated too! GRATITUDE is the key to living your dreams!

As I Ponder...

You've done everything except DEAL WITH IT! Not forgiving blocks manifestation! Could that be your delay?

The beauty of this journey called life is that everybody and I mean EVERYBODY gets a turn! Prepare now, because when it's time to produce you won't have time to prepare! Are you REALLY ready for what you say you want?

To deny pleasure is to perpetually journey to a place where you eventually feel NOTHING! Have some fun and get your life back!

What Stirs in My Spirit Is ...

While pain is powerful, pleasure is transformative!

Faith is NON-SENSE! It goes against all that you know and perceive with your senses! (Gotcha didn't I?)

As I Reflect ...

Church DOGMA makes people lie! Kingdom principles create a safe space for honesty and truth and GROWTH! Stop the madness.

The way to manifest your miracle is to help create a miracle for someone else!

Just woke up thanking God for all the things I asked for and He told me NO! Man, what was I thinking? (LOL)

As I Ponder...

Pain is God's reminder to constantly re-evaluate WHO and WHAT really matters in the big picture. Clarity is...priceless!

When engaged in its purest form, love has revolutionary potential! People don't make the world go round - LOVE (the way God intended) does! Try it and enjoy the results!

I don't have to DO anything as much as I have to BE-lieve (agree, align with) what has already been created for me! Just BE and let God DO through you!

What Stirs in My Spirit Is ...

There IS a place in God where you become so full of Him that people can't tell where you end and He begins! He's keeping me alive!

I'm so glad I don't have to be God. I can just activate the God in me to make it through the tough times.

The risk of loving deeply is hurting deeply too! (In memory of Dr. Geraldine "Mom" McInnis)

As I Reflect ...

Chapter 4

Movement is critical to the flow of LIFE! SCREAMING this - if it ain't moving - it is DYING!

I don't - TRUST ME - look like what I've been through! God's been just THAT mmm mmm good!

Life is about choices in THAT moment! Your next move is critical!

As I Ponder...

God gives grace for what He requires. If you don't have the grace (tolerance, acceptance, patience, passion) then maybe God is not requiring it of you. Just something to think about....

Ladies we attract what we reflect! Think about it honestly. Our relationships mirror our strengths AND our weak spots. It's imperative that we become a WHOLE cherry, apple, peach or whatever PIE; so that we don't keep joining ourselves to A SLICE. Once you realize that you're FULLfilled, then comes the WHIPPED or ICE CREAM that adds to your already sweet flavor. Happy Baking!

Stop wasting energy and time resisting what's resisting you. Simply go with the flow - it's much easier - and it is REALLY that simple!

What Stirs in My Spirit Is ...

Extraordinary people simply do a little extra! They keep going when others simply quit!

Give YOUR man a safe and peaceful place to lay his head; appeal to his senses and then enjoy the results! Notice I said YOUR man! Bishop T. D. Jakes says, "Samson didn't fall because he was lustful, he landed in Delilah's lap because he was TIRED!" (Ding, ding, ding, ding, ding!) That's the bell of insight ringing!

Dreams come true and nightmares do too! In other words, think happy thoughts before you go to sleep.

As I Reflect ...

If you expect a mess, mistrust, or misuse - that is what you'll get. Likewise, if you expect a miracle - you'll get that too! (Wink)

If you don't have a deep understanding about what's REALLY going on, then MIND YOUR OWN BUSINESS; lest you end up serving a life sentence for something that had NOTHING to do with YOU! I'm just saying.....

As I Ponder...

No matter what, find joy in it!

I believe I can do anything; or I can believe it's not gonna work - EITHER way I am right! Whatever you believe you become!

Don't be so quick to reject what you haven't explored; it just may be the answer you've been waiting for!

What Stirs in My Spirit Is ...

(Exhaling slowly) Ladies, if we would RELAX and stand down, then our men will RESPOND and stand up! Girl, let him be THE MAN! (Rolling my eyes up in my head.)

TRUE SURRENDER is the victim in you giving into the victor in you! Got that one while I was asleep - whew! Surrender to the victor within!

What do you REALLY want? I mean REALLY? Thoughts become things...are you thinking about what you REALLY want?

As I Reflect ...

It doesn't matter what has happened in your life up to this point. Play to the end because ANYTHING is possible! IT is within your reach and beyond your imagination...Now is the time to GO FOR IT!

Rare but extremely refreshing to meet someone who REALLY is who they say they are! Who are you?

As I Ponder...

Don't let other people's CRAZY mess up your day! Tell them now - you are just NOT going to do it!

You have the absolute right and freedom to be like you are! Question HOW'S THAT WORKING FOR YOU? Just asking.

It's simple...say what you want THEN live like you have it!

What Stirs in My Spirit Is ...

When it seems impossible with man know that God has a plan and is working it ALL out! You can receive at least one ridiculous miracle a day!

I mean really - what are you waiting for? Don't wait until you die to live again! Start now!

Engage EVERY moment because any moment can be THE moment!

As I Reflect ...

Chapter 5

We always live at CHOICE! You don't HAVE to do anything!

QUESTION: If it is not working for you (and you KNOW it is not) - why are you so committed to it?

GIVE ME THAT BLANKET LINUS! It's okay! I'm trying to give you something better; -not leave you uncovered!

As I Ponder...

Peace like the kind that can flood a soul comes from seeking to UNDERSTAND rather than be UNDERSTOOD!

I remind you again, if you don't have a dream, how are you going to have a dream come true? Thoughts become things - AH HAH!

What Stirs in My Spirit Is ...

Quitting is NOT an option - keep moving!

There's nothing like living in the NO FEAR ZONE. I love it here! (Hint: Perfect love casts out ALL fear!)

We can be SO used to struggle that when life becomes easy we don't believe it! BELIEVE IT - your struggle is over loved one! Relax!

As I Reflect ...

He whispered in a still, small voice, "Just because you don't see me doing it doesn't mean I'm not doing it!" He speaks the same to you.

TRUE FREEDOM is knowing I don't HAVE to do anything...it's always MY choice. You are where you want to be. If you don't like it - change it!

I don't have to look like the middle because I have an expected end! I'm gonna reflect what I believe the end to be - BETTER!

As I Ponder...

Champions produce in the light what they prepare for in obscurity! Trust me; I don't look like what I've been through.

If you're going to play in the game - think like a champion or get off the court!

When the WHY becomes powerful enough...the HOW becomes easy!

What Stirs in My Spirit Is ...

Be FULLY present in EVERY moment because the NEXT moment can change your life FOREVER!

Double check - When fearlessness connects with unshakable faith your life experiences will reflect a season of resurrection and ascension!

Fear is the root of religious and political dogma, divorce, distorted imaginations, and damaged lives! Fear can kiss my ass!

As I Reflect ...

When you finally settle into BE-ing, the DO-ing will automatically follow with ease!

We are not afraid of failure as much as we feel unworthy of success! THAT IS MISINFORMATION - go for it without guilt or regret!

When things look impossible to man, that's when God performs His BEST and most unforgettable interventions! I BELIEVE GOD IS THE GREATEST POWER!

As I Ponder...

The peace, love, and contentment you seek come from nourishing your soul and silencing your ego!

When folks are talking a lot but not saying much, one of the greatest gifts you can give yourself is a MUTE button!

You have NOTHING to fear! NOTHING! Fear won't keep you from dying but it sure will keep you from living!

What Stirs in My Spirit Is ...

It's a waste of good love, time, and energy to be in a relationship and never RELATE! If we can't spend TIME together we won't be together - PERIOD!

If you ask for, seek, and desire LOVE, but you expect, wait, and prepare for heartbreak - SHIFT NOW! Why? Because you get what you prepare for not what you expect!

As I Reflect ...

I LOVE WHO I GET TO BE IN THE WORLD! I had the opportunity to spend the day with NeoSoul recording artists Marsha Ambrosius and Melonie Fiona! THEY are going to have LONG careers - just humble, down-to-earth, talented, beautiful, grateful- for-the-chance kind of WOMEN who didn't give up! Keep pressing; YOUR turn is coming if you just stay in line and stop being so restless. When you are ready the doors will open! BE PATIENT!

Trust and follow the voice of your HEART! It's when we listen to the chatter of other body parts <side eye> that we only get to experience some instead of all that the dream entails!

If you want wealth, wholeness, and wellness, STOP declaring how broke, sick and tired you are. Live in ACTIVE gratitude for your abundance!

As I Ponder...

Trust the process - especially when it doesn't make sense! That's when God does His BEST work!

Standing in the gap and being a bridge when the one you love feels crippled by fear, pain, and doubt - that's LOVE! Being a quiet, safe, and patient refuge in times of turmoil - that's LOVE too! LOVE is what LOVE DOES!

When you live in the ABYSS OF INDECISION the root cause is fear. Unfortunately, you spend a lot of time doing nothing, going nowhere, meeting no one, and feeling like nobody! Choose LOVE and get moving again!

What Stirs in My Spirit Is ...

Life is happening NOW, whether you engage it or not. Don't miss the moments of LOVE (yes, everything is love) because of past pain or future fear! The present is a PRESENT!

Now what IS normal and attractive is an attitude of gratitude, a peaceful and gentle spirit, an abundance of humility, a joyful and charming presence, a smiling face, an open heart, and the intention to LOVE THE HELL OUT OF PEOPLE!

Your perpetual turmoil, stress, distress, anger, drama, funky attitude, frowned up face and fear based tantrums are NOT NORMAL and NOT ATTRACTIVE! You might not be able to change what has happened to you but you can certainly change how you CHOOSE to respond to it!

As I Reflect ...

Chapter 6

Too often we judge and condemn what we know nothing about based on assumptions and our own fears! Whether it's another person, our own dreams and desires, sexuality, or life in general - in all of your getting information - GET SOME UNDERSTANDING FIRST - then talk!

We tolerate the level of abuse from others that we inflict upon ourselves! Likewise, we receive the level of love from others that we AUTHENTICALLY shower upon ourselves.

Love makes one a person of: responsibility, humility, accountability, peace, abundance and selflessness. Maybe that's why so many CHOOSE to live in patterns/cycles of chaos, ego, drama, turmoil, indecision, guilt and clutter - foolishness requires nothing from you!

As I Ponder...

If you would just be your AUTHENTIC, LOVING SELF you wouldn't have to sneak, hide, lie, pretend, deceive, hurt others, and abuse self and others in the first doggone place! BE HEALED so you can stop the pain!

We must stop covering up what should be exposed and stop exposing what should be covered. It's called INTEGRITY and DISCRETION!

Church as we know it is NOT church the way God intended! When the Body of Christ stops acting like church is a country club- then "WHOSOEVER" will not only come visit but they will stay awhile!

What Stirs in My Spirit Is ...

Where you are is NOT all there is! You don't have to live another day addicted to lack, poverty, struggle, or counterfeit love! Any takers for NEXT LEVEL LIVING? Make your declaration here__________________.

Reconfiguring my LIFE to align with the RESTORATION in progress! Thank you to any and every one who EVER hurt me, betrayed me, caused me pain. You played your role superbly and THIS IS YOUR LAST ACKNOWLEDGEMENT!

The pain of disaster, turmoil, and universal suffering is a tremendous equalizer! LOVE IS TOO! (Hint)

As I Reflect ...

I had a moment of reflection as I said goodbye in 2011 to a great man, my Uncle Chuck. Here's what the moment taught me; live so that when you die, the works you've done speak for you!

The illusion of importance is one thing! True fulfillment however, is when your impact exceeds the image you've worked so hard to maintain. HELP SOMEBODY AND DON'T TELL ANYBODY!

The power of God is ENERGY IN MOTION! I prophetically declare that after you dance to the jam that moves you - you will experience an UNEXPECTED, NOTICEABLE MIRACLE in your life! It's only for those who BELIEVE that GOD IS THE GREATEST POWER! I dare you to EXPECT THE GREAT!

As I Ponder...

Inner conflict is much worse than external opposition because you will be with you wherever you go! Deal with your ISH so you can stop creating unnecessary turmoil!

There is no compulsion, force, self-hatred, fear, guilt, or hard work in authentic living! DOING YOU SHOULD BE EASY! If you don't like what you see when you look in the mirror or how you feel - get rid of, let go of and resist anything that disrupts your peace or blocks your flow!

If you can't live YOUR truth out loud without justification, introduction, or disclaimers - then maybe it doesn't belong to you. TRUTH JUST IS and needs no explanation!

What Stirs in My Spirit Is ...

If you become LOVE then you'll always have LOVE and won't have to look for LOVE. You will not act crazy or compromise for LOVE because you will be LOVE and attract what you are reflecting!

The beauty of a butterfly is exposed AFTER its process is completed as a caterpillar. Locked within your pain is a promise full of joy and pleasure unimaginable! Be encouraged butterfly, the process IS working!

You knew it was raining BEFORE you went out in it. Sing or dance in it now! Don't get mad because I didn't give you an umbrella. Oh, but know this, when you come in from the rain - a nice warm towel will be waiting!

As I Reflect ...

Be easy and gentle with yourself. Life is hard enough already without your help!

If you want to live and BE a certain way, you must THINK and talk a certain way! Your life right now is a reflection of YOUR thoughts! Hmmmm...

You can't earn worthiness! It's already yours. Embrace it!

As I Ponder...

It costs to care! So, choose wisely where you invest emotional, mental, physical, and financial resources lest you end up bankrupt! Have you checked your CARE BUDGET lately!

It really amazes me when people proclaim they want to go somewhere else or do something different but refuse and resist leaving where they are.

Insecurity rises to the surface when surrounded by significance! You have no need to fight JUST BE YOUR SIGNIFICANT SELF. The atmosphere will shift because YOU are there!

What Stirs in My Spirit Is ...

Be as fabulous, wonderful, sexy, handsome, insightful, and intelligent in real life as you are on social networks! Meeting the real you shouldn't be disappointing!

At the end of the day, people don't want to keep hearing how much you've suffered! People want to hear how you survived!

The intimate nature of my experiences with God has PERPETUALLY positioned me in a realm where impossibilities are now possible. Being loved like this should be a crime but it is not - It's a Fantastic Voyage!

As I Reflect ...

There is NO HONOR in suffering silently and NO SHAME in asking for help! Healing is available to everyone for anything - PERIOD!

Your resistance creates more of what you don't want! Conversely, when you just surrender, ALLOW what is to be and flow, what you really want will manifest! Try it!

When you do the last thing God told you to do THEN He'll tell you what's next! You've gotta trust Him on this one!

As I Ponder...

YOU must confront whatever it is in you that has you so committed to being miserable! If you're not willing to work on it and CHANGE then STOP COMPLAINING!

When God allows a door to be shut He ALWAYS leaves a window open somewhere close for you to see tomorrow's opportunity! Get yourself together and go look!

While I will not work hard to be in a relationship, I will be consistent, committed, caring, compassionate, and resolve conflict quickly, while continuing to be the best me to bring out the BEST IN YOU!

What Stirs in My Spirit Is ...

I know what the song says and I disagree. I can make you love me if you don't! However, I don't feel like working that hard anymore SO - your loss!

STOP IT! Stop complaining, whining, instigating, procrastinating, worrying, nagging, manipulating, and sabotaging! STOP IT! We suffer according to the level of drama we create to feel significant! YOU ARE LOVEABLE WITHOUT THE FOOLISHNESS!

YOU are not in control - God is. So allow the process to work (resistance makes it worse and delays your coming out of it). In other words, everything that falls apart ALWAYS falls into place as you surrender!

As I Reflect ...

Chapter 7

Don't be alarmed or too anxious by the interruptions, disruptions, or delays! God is breaking your routine and casting you into the realm of the UNUSUAL! How else were you going to get to BETTER?

I know you don't understand the why of IT - but IT had to happen just like that. IT is going to work in your favor!

Your next step is ALREADY ready for you. Time is waiting for you to get ready for that place! So relax, EVERYTHING happens when and the way it's supposed to!

When fear and terror knock on your door - ummmm, DON'T OPEN IT! They only have power to run your house when you let them in!

As I Ponder...

You prayed! God answered! Show, do, be LOVE - it works eventually - every time!

Make sure you put just as much LOVE into the other 364 days of the year as you put into February 14th!

I'm walking out God's intention for my life (in the sunshine) not man's interpretation of what they think it should be!

What Stirs in My Spirit Is ...

The worst is over! The ending of THAT is the beginning of BETTER!

When you get sick and tired of being in bondage, you'll change - BY ANY MEANS NECESSARY!

It's better to be whole, happy and alone, than to be broken into pieces daily by someone who doesn't value their access to you!

Follow PEACE - literally! Wherever peace goes, you go! When peace leaves - YOU LEAVE!

As I Reflect ...

Sometimes all you can do is ALL you can do!

SOMETIMES your breakthrough takes a little longer than others because you are being prepared for multi--directional and long-term success! God is working even when you can't see Him moving!

WE ATTRACT WHAT WE REFLECT! Soooo, if you want to attract Mr. Right then become Ms. Right and vice versa! If you keep attracting what you don't like then YOU have some work to do!

As I Ponder...

Don't act like IT didn't happen - IT did! Face it, feel it fully, and while you're moving forward IT will be fixed!

Make a DIFFERENCE or not; and then you die! Thing is, if you choose not to live a life of impact you're already dead! Work the "-" so people won't have to make up something to say about you!

Be intentional and aware in every moment! Idle words, careless choices, and sleepwalking through life are going to write a check you won't be able to cash - leaving you emotionally, spiritually, mentally, and relationally bankrupt!

What Stirs in My Spirit Is ...

Your DEVOTION opens your life's treasures!

A woman intrinsically wants a man to be a LEADER not a ruler! There's a difference. When a man is walking in his true KINGMANSHIP, women relish the opportunity to be his Queen! Submit, surrender, support, suggest, and surround a woman with LOVE- Hmmmm - it's easy from there - BE A WOMAN'S HERO and HER HEART WILL FOLLOW!

While love can be enjoyed within an exclusive context, it should never be RESTRICTIVE! That's a crucial mistake that many people make! Real love is about FREEDOM!

As I Reflect ...

I feel like keeping it light today and laughing as much as possible (which I do everyday anyway). Laughter is BETTER than medicine!

When a woman taps into her worth, she unlocks unrestrained favor, influence, passion, and ummmm pleasure!

What do sad people have in common? It seems they have all built a shrine to the past and often go there to do a strange wail and worship. What is the beginning of happiness? To stop being so religious!

When you start honoring your truth, other people will start honoring you! Living a lie so other people will feel good is MADNESS!

As I Ponder...

Excuses are equal opportunity dream killers! Get rid of them!

Just because you've been through the fire doesn't mean you have to spend the rest of your life smelling like smoke! Change your clothes and be glad you didn't die in the blaze! KEEP MOVING FORWARD... you can do this!

What Stirs in My Spirit Is ...

Your suffering has shaped your life long enough! STOP IT! From this moment forward allow your pleasure, joy, peace, fun to give you an extreme makeover!

When we release our attachment to the superficial and self-serving, we'll begin to experience and enjoy authentic relationships!

You must confront whatever it is in you that has you so invested in being miserable! Once it's confronted it can be corrected!

As I Reflect ...

Chapter 8

Get away QUICKLY from people who are comfortable in their perpetual madness and then give you all the pain and consequences to deal with and manage!

My daughter, at 17 posed, "We don't know our history! Seems like slavery still exists today except now it is just in our minds! Huh?"

Everything is not for everybody! Just because it makes you uncomfortable doesn't make it wrong for others. Conversely, just because it's comfortable for you doesn't make it right for others. The real question is: how's that working for you?

If Jesus came that we might have life more abundantly, why are so many churched people broke, sick, unhappy, lonely, emotionally numb, tired, horny, and just plain miserable? (Shoulder shrug)

As I Ponder...

Fear of intimacy will cause people to seek relationship without responsibility, payoff without process, access without attachment, and companionship without commitment! I AM A NO FEAR ZONE! (Inspired by Lance Watson)

Lust is really love choked by fear! Authentic love awakens your senses and sensibility to the point that lust won't be necessary!

If you are in pain for ANY reason and want relief, open up and start loving! Kirk Nugent (an amazing light in the earth) put it this way, the love you withhold is the pain you carry!

What Stirs in My Spirit Is ...

Pastor Ford Huskey preached: The Good News is The Bad News is NOT True! With all the odds stacked against you Honey, God has the LAST say so! Not guilty! Not having it! Not here!

Drama, manipulation, conflict, jealousy, anxiety and neediness are the results of fear-based loving! If you want the opposite, surrender to and trust the beauty of your fearlessness!

I believe every day can be the start of a year of upsets, u-turns, and unbelievable victories! Underdogs REJOICE!

As I Reflect ...

A good teacher imparts knowledge but a GREAT teacher imparts the joy of learning!

While you're behind the wheel of your life - watch the distractions! A split second decision to SHIFT can be the difference between a side swipe and a head-on collision!

We don't realize how hard we are working to love and be loved until someone comes along and does it authentically and effortlessly.

As I Ponder...

Where a man puts his TIME is where his heart is! The gifts, the sex, the money, the occasional overnight stays are simply evidence that you're only in his head (both of them)!

Moving forward spend the most time where you are celebrated and motivated; not tolerated, berated, or hated! YOU HAVE NOTHING TO PROVE!

Motivational PowerhouseTony Robbins said, "Most people aren't happy, but they're not unhappy enough to do anything about it! And that's a dangerous place to be." Wow! How much more of your time are you going to give to things, people, and stuff that are not working for you?

What Stirs in My Spirit Is ...

Ladies if you act like or look like a man he will treat you like one! Just because you can, doesn't mean you should. Our STRENGTH is found in what many misunderstand to be weakness - it's called feminine pulchritude!

God believes in YOU!

It's a WONDERFUL thing when the unusual infiltrates the usual and makes a difference! Ahhhhh…

As I Reflect ...

Please join me as I expect a miracle EVERYDAY for the rest of my life! Anyone accepting my invitation?

Don't you be bound by OTHER PEOPLE'S limitations!

As you move forward please take your thinking with you lest you go in CIRCLES!

As I Ponder...

Wherever you are, whatever you are doing, however you are feeling IS YOUR CHOICE! I'm happy with my choices - are you?

If you ever watch the Sunday NFL action, then you have witnessed the power of a STRONG FINISH! That's what really counts - when it is all over!

Wanting better is not enough! You must SHIFT what you believe is possible. You don't get what you deserve, desire or wish for necessarily. I can guarantee however, that you always get what you expect!

What Stirs in My Spirit Is ...

When people show you who they are take a picture and then decide if you want to frame it and give it a special place on a ledge in your life or NOT!

Self-examination requires tremendous amounts of self-love without judgment. When you discover the imperfections - LOVE THAT PART TOO!

It is the things we MOST dislike in others that we really loathe about ourselves. Hence the encouragement to be KIND, LOVING, and GENTLE with you first; only then can you love others unconditionally!

As I Reflect ...

Chapter 9

If you're not attracting what you want where you are - here's a simple suggestion: GO SOME PLACE ELSE! Hit REFRESH today!

We attract what we reflect! So if you're attracting things/people that DON'T feel good it's a sure sign you're not being good to yourself! HIT RESET!

If there are things in your life that are still crippling you and it's been YEARS - you may need more than prayer, praise, speaking in tongues, laying on of hands, and a weekly word! YOU NEED THERAPY!

As I Ponder...

HERE'S THE SECRET - When you genuinely give it ALL (love, gentleness, kindness, fun, honesty, peace) to yourself first then you begin to attract people into your life to share it with!

Maybe your life is HALF HAPPY because you do too many things HALF way!

Believing is stronger than hoping! KNOWING is stronger than believing! Elevate your options and you'll upgrade your life!

What Stirs in My Spirit Is ...

The older I get the CLEARER things become! Difficult people who like drama and suffering get nothing from me but a loving BLANK STARE!

Determination and SMART work equals success!

Real prosperity doesn't begin with what's in your wallet or your bank account, it starts with your heart then your mind and then manifests in your life!

As I Reflect ...

Just one moment of letting go, not needing to have all the answers, an instant of trust and self-love INSTANTLY changes everything!

People who waddle in the darkness of their own suffering will have a hard time being happy for the light of your joy! Keep it moving Beloved - it's not personal!

Celebrate your success in detail with the people who supported your struggle in detail. That way you'll avoid the bootleg sentiment and people in your life for selfish gain!

As I Ponder...

You don't need approval of your choices especially from people who can't make healthy choices in their own lives!

Laziness does NOT produce transformation! Stop complaining about your life especially if you have no intention of shifting; and go find some joy in your humdrumness!

When you are consumed by your past and fearful of the future, you're guaranteed to mismanage the blessing of RIGHT NOW!

What Stirs in My Spirit Is ...

What I love about Jesus standing over the woman caught in adultery is how He challenged (lovingly dared) her accusers to stone her in FRONT OF HIM. Make a right turn and walk away before you get exposed too!

If you SAY you're going to do something then do it! If you don't keep your word in simple things - it's a good chance the rest of your life LACKS integrity too!

If you only accumulate money to get things and status but never work on who you are as a person, you are still an impoverished soul! AUTHENTIC WEALTH IS AN INSIDE JOB!

As I Reflect ...

Loved Ones - please stop asking broke people how to make money; wounded people how to feel better, lazy people how to do better, and miserable people how to be happy!

Everything (and I do mean EVERY thing) that has happened in your life up to this moment has prepared you for the GLORY that comes after the shame!

It doesn't matter how many people are against you. All you need is one person to believe in and be for you!

As I Ponder...

Now that you're on your way UP, call and say thank you to someone who loved you when you were down!

You're waiting on some things to happen so you can move forward in life and those same things are waiting on you to SHOW UP so they can see you!

When people have INNER AUTHORITY they don't abuse, mishandle, or confuse their outer and expressed authority! Be careful how you treat people when you have a li'l power; the boomerang is not discerning!

What Stirs in My Spirit Is ...

Love is like oxygen - go without it too long - you'll suffocate!

Don't put your joy, fun, dreams, life and pursuit of happiness on hold waiting for other people to approve and/or to decide to join you. LIVE FULLY NOW; either they'll join you, catch up to you or they won't!

It's time to shift your mourning to morning! You've endured a lot - now it's time to IN(side)-JOY your life!

As I Reflect ...

Chapter 10

People spend so much time worrying about what if, what's not, and what might happen that they neglect to enjoy what IS and what CAN be!

Resisting, despising, resenting the journey diminishes the joy of and delays the arrival of what you're waiting for! Life is hard enough - BE EASY ON YOURSELF!

Even when it looks like I missed my goal; and even in those times when I come close yet still miss my goal - I CONTINUE TO BELIEVE that what's mine is for me and that God's timing is so perfect it will be like I got there when I thought I should have been there!

As I Ponder...

Don't wait to get what you want to be happy! BE HAPPY ANYWAY and the desires of your heart will just show up to add to your already blissful living!

It doesn't matter what you desire, intend, hope for, dream about, want, declare, decree, work hard for, demand, pray for, name or claim belongs to you in Jesus name - YOU GET WHAT YOU EXPECT! Hmmmmm....

Be careful how you treat others when you are the big fish in a small pond. The true measure of your influence and impact on others is how you thrive (or not) when you have to swim in the ocean with other big fish!

What Stirs in My Spirit Is ...

When you're willing to risk losing it all to keep your integrity intact is the moment you have proven that you're ready to have it all!

If the wait was long, service poor, food bad and expensive - you wouldn't go back to that restaurant now would you? Take care of your HEART the same way - stop giving access to people who don't know how to treat you!

If things are going to change in your life - YOU HAVE TO MAKE A DECISION and CHANGE THEM! Waiting on others to change so things will be different for you is futile.

As I Reflect ...

GET UP so you can GO UP! Before you can transcend (get beyond it) you must ascend (rise above it) to fully heal and mend the fractured pieces of your life!

There is a fierce urgency and magnificent power in RIGHT NOW! The moment you're waiting for may or may not happen if you keep delaying. Do IT now!

Serve the way you want to be served! Give the way you want to receive! Love the way you want to be loved! Good measure, pressed down, shaken together, running over will it come back to you!

As I Ponder...

Here's the thing Beloved - the promise ALWAYS just shows up while you're busy becoming and evolving into a BETTER PERSON! Focus on your person not the promise!

Just as the rainbow ever so gently peaks through after the rain, so will your promise after the pain! Everything is ALREADY alright and all right!

The power of making ADULT DECISIONS repeatedly is what fuels us to stop acting like wounded children in adult bodies! It's your choice how far you go or not!

One of the most valuable keys to success is finding a way to say YES instead of looking for reasons to say no! Your YES releases the next detail!

What Stirs in My Spirit Is ...

Gotta love how when ALL odds are against you - somehow - things ALWAYS even out in your favor!

Your transformation transforms everything around you! You're waiting on God and God is waiting on YOU to release what you ALREADY have! (Translation: make the shift, the change, the choice. GET ON WITH IT!)

Frequently, the miracle or answer to your prayer is right in front of you simply waiting for your recognition. LOOK AGAIN!

As I Reflect ...

If I have to convince you to love me, perform for you to love me, lose me for you to love me, be lied to for you to love me, accept scraps while you give your best to others for you to love me - KEEP IT - that's control - not love!

Authentic love does not force, manipulate, deceive, orchestrate, violate, or bamboozle. AUTHENTIC LOVE ALLOWS WHAT IS TO BE and WHAT'S NOT - TO BE AS WELL!

Sometimes the most loving thing you can do for people is not to grace them with your presence, but empower them with your absence!

As I Ponder...

Dig up the weeds in your life from the root (go deep) and deal with them - lest when it's time for you to blossom your success will be choked to death by the very weeds you refused to get rid of.

If you're sitting at someone's table and they refuse to feed you or only give you scraps - don't just sit there and starve. GET UP! Somebody - somewhere - is waiting to serve you a full course, gourmet, nutritious meal!

PRIORITY access is not free. As a matter of fact, it's quite expensive! Stop letting people ride in the first class section of your life when in fact they really only paid for a buddy pass!

What Stirs in My Spirit Is ...

What's going on in your life right now is not forever! Pull yourself together, gather the pieces that still work and keep it moving. WHAT YOU HAVE LEFT IS ENOUGH. Too often people give their all to protecting an image that's NOT working for them. STOP THAT FOOLISHNESS! If you need help - ASK! If you don't know - ASK! If you're not sure - ASK! It's the self-loving thing to do!

Just like we're conditioned to suffer, we can be conditioned NOT to suffer! How do you know it won't work when you haven't tried it?

As I Reflect ...

Every now and then you just have to STOP and deal with your stuff! The reality is if you don't - eventually, your stuff is going to deal with you and it won't be pretty! Be proactive - not reactive!

Whenever you're continually blocked from being included behind-the-scenes - it's a STRONG indication that you're being pushed to CENTER STAGE! Stop acting like a groupie and step into the spotlight!

As I Ponder...

I speak the language of the life I desire to have - even if what you SEE is not what I'm saying! Know that I am just catching up to who I ALREADY AM!

DREAM anyway! When the odds are against you - DREAM anyway! When it looks like the sun won't shine again - DREAM anyway! For you single parents who sacrifice and sacrifice for your children - DREAM anyway!

Integrity preserves you! It involves your character, ability to exercise restraint and most importantly what you say! BE IMPECCABLE WITH YOUR WORDS! If you don't mean it - don't say it! If you make a promise - keep it! When you tell the truth - YOU DON'T HAVE TO HIDE!

What Stirs in My Spirit Is ...

Do something constructive with your negatively charged emotions. Don't just wallow in them! Anger turned inward and unexpressed is DEPRESSION! Anger released in a healthy way is the energy of CHANGE!

What you're waiting for is waiting on you to make room to receive it properly! MORE will NOT show up to be mistreated! When you're ready for success - success is ready for you!

A poverty mentality doesn't always ONLY mean you don't have. It also means you CONSTANTLY overlook opportunity because you're used to the struggle!

As I Reflect ...

Chapter 11

When your prayers AVAIL it's time to PREVAIL! In other words, do something with the answer when it shows up!

If you can't or choose not to give it everything - then don't give it anything! This is the essence of purpose-driven living!

Being able to lovingly release people from your life is a sign that you're on your way to the MASTERY OF LOVE!

As I Ponder...

It's not always easy to embrace but once you do it's simple! When you adjust your beliefs, attitude, and posture, WHAT YOU'RE LOOKING FOR BEGINS TO PASSIONATELY PURSUE YOU!

LOVE doesn't require that we self-destruct; self sacrifice to the point of having nothing left! WHEN LOVING THEM IS KILLING YOU - SAVE YOURSELF! You can't give away what you don't have! You know what they tell you on the plane – right? PUT ON YOUR OXYGEN MASK BEFORE YOU ATTEMPT TO ASSIST ANOTHER PASSENGER!

A "no" from one person doesn't prevent a "yes" from the next five! Stop being faint-hearted and giving up so easily! You're a WINNER - act like it!

What Stirs in My Spirit Is ...

Whether it's the game of basketball, football, tennis or the game of life - you can't wish to win - you must SHOW UP FIRST and then PLAY to win!

Accepting what God allows will make you cry sometimes - but it will ALWAYS make you better!

It's going to hurt more to stay the same than it will if you take the risk to make some necessary life changes!

As I Reflect ...

Being afraid can work FOR or AGAINST you! You can be scared not to change or you can be so scared that you don't change! I suggest you CHOOSE to CHANGE ANYWAY!

Awareness, consciousness, spiritual growth and maturity are all the SAME THING! There can be no real change if you live your life as a SPIRITUAL ROBOT.

When you don't stand in the FULLness of who God is in you, you cause those attached to your greatness to play small too! STAND UP STRAIGHT!

As I Ponder...

Rejoice when people tell you it can't be done! It just means you have one less person to impress!

The moment you realize that God has made YOU the answer you'll stop being so consumed and driven by the problem!

When people SEARCH for significance they often SETTLE for anything that often equates to - not much! CLUE: You already HAVE what you're looking for!

What Stirs in My Spirit Is ...

Live so fully that when you die - you're empty!

Just because I'm not saying anything does not mean I don't see it!

When you have an employee mindset other people have access to pull your strings! When you have the mind of an ENTREPRENEUR - you design the strings!

As I Reflect ...

Compulsive church work is not Kingdom building just like running your mouth is not exercise!

Stay open to CHANGE - your next miracle will come through the unlikely, the unknown, and the uncommon!

You do NOT need approval from others to honor choices that make YOUR soul smile!

As I Ponder...

Unconditional consistency is a trait of TRUE friendship!

Give yourself the gift of healing and self-love! Thing is - you can't give away what you don't have and more importantly, no one wants a SICK DOCTOR telling them how to get better!

What Stirs in My Spirit Is ...

Some people actually prefer emotional captivity, spiritual bondage or mental struggle because they feel it justifies their reckless living! Well I'm telling you it does NOT and simply put - GROW UP and OUT OF IT!

Please be heart full and honestly examine the things you ask for! WHY? Because after you get it you may find you didn't really want THAT like that after all.

Inhale and exhale the freshness of God today overstanding (not understanding) that anything that did not or does not feel good can now be classified as EX-hell!

As I Reflect ...

Chapter 12

If you REALLY want something - but don't invest the time to learn HOW to get it - you're just wishing and guaranteed to REALLY get nothing!

THE STRUGGLE IS OVER! It's time to live in the EASE of God!

Just because I'm FOR me doesn't make me against you! Please stop apologizing for being who you are! There's enough for everyone to shine when you FULLY show up!

As I Ponder...

When it seems that everything and almost everyone is against you (there's always at least one person somewhere in your corner - STOP that mind trip right now), it's a sure sign that God is FOR YOU!

Make the shift in your mind and heart RIGHT NOW from selfish to selfless - there is a gift inside of you that the world is waiting for you to release!

One thing we all will come to know by choice or by force - GOD IS SO MUCH BIGGER THAN THE BOX WE HAVE HIM IN!

What Stirs in My Spirit Is ...

Truth - especially when spoken in love - can be like the worst tasting medicine - unpleasant in the short-term but a lifesaver in the long run!

You can hold on to it if you want to, but for those of you who are really ready to release it THE STRUGGLE IS OVER! (Drops mic and exits stage right!)

You're going to give up and do what? Quit and win how? If you're weary then rest, get refreshed and get back out there! CHAMPIONS are usually the people who kept going when everyone else gave up!

As I Reflect ...

People believe what they SEE; not so much what you say! Therefore, it is more important to under-commit and over-deliver with excellence than to over-commit and under-deliver with excuses!

What God is doing with you has NEVER been done before so stop comparing, competing, and contending with other people! Take courage with you and DO IT!

As I Ponder...

Today I decided from deep within my heart that the rest of my life is going to look like a soul-filled, purpose-filled, fun-filled vacation!

We all were created for multidirectional success - not unilateral mediocrity just enough to get by living! Spread those eggs around. If you don't, you're waiting on something that won't ever happen!

Caring and Loving are not the same thing. Care without love is dangerously costly to your overall well being. It costs to care. It pays to love. CARE LESS and LOVE MORE.

What Stirs in My Spirit Is ...

When you constantly add unnecessary variables (i.e. other people's opinions) to the equation of YOUR life's choices, you only delay the manifestation of what you ALREADY know to do. TRUST and FOLLOW YOUR HEART!

You're too close to the moment to quit now. KEEP SHOWING UP! What you're looking for is looking for you. Keep going - you can do this!

If you're being stretched beyond what's reasonable - please know that it's because the blessings headed your way are UNREASONABLE, UNEXPECTED, and UNBELIEVABLY worth e-v-e-r-y-t-h-i-n-g you've endured!

If many of us spent half as much time investing in becoming a better person or building REAL relationships as we do on social media, texting, and other technology - the quality of our lives would be exponentially increased!

As I Reflect ...

Sometimes it takes years and years of BELIEVING; even when it seems like nothing is happening! Then - IT happens!

When my daughter was about 9 years old she asked, “Mommy, if burdens are heavy, why do adults carry them around?” Her question still jolts me some. Become CHILD-LIKE again; trust that ANYTHING is possible if you BELIEVE!

Stop reacting, responding, returning to what was, resisting, regretting, regressing, and giving up and in, because you think it’s over! THIS is just one chapter - FINISH THE REST OF THE STORY - you choose the ending - MAKE IT GOOD!

As I Ponder...

At the end of the day, at the end of your life -the ONLY thing that will really matter is how many people knew that you genuinely, fully, deeply LOVED them!

When someone REALLY loves you they add to your life not subtract from it; they multiply your joy not divide it into pieces; they build you up not tear you down; they give you energy not drain you. REAL LOVE MAKES YOU FEEL LIKE YOU CAN TOUCH THE SKY!

Frustration is an indication that it's time to do something DIFFERENT!

What Stirs in My Spirit Is ...

Sometimes people make it very easy not to like them and unnecessarily hard to love them! CUT IT OUT! You're blocking your blessings!

The moment you BELIEVE what you expect and EXPECT what you believe - things begin to happen in your favor IMMEDIATELY!

Many people are so CONFORMED to their struggle and suffering that it's difficult (not impossible) to perceive, hear, engage opportunity when it knocks on their door.

As I Reflect ...

You are not what happened to you! Start celebrating your BREAKTHROUGHS and stop memorializing your breakdowns! That story is OLD NEWS!

Vision is looking at what others say can't or won't be done, asking WHY NOT? Then declaring in your heart and with your actions (not your words) - WATCH ME!

As I Ponder...

A champion THRIVES anyway and somehow finds a way to turn pain into power - misery and mistakes into a personal mission - failures into fruitfulness! AWAY WITH THE EXCUSES! EVERYBODY IS GOING THROUGH SOMETHING!

The love of God is to cover us while we WORK ON OUR ISSUES; not to hide behind and use as an excuse not to be authentic and productive!

What Stirs in My Spirit Is ...

When you SEE love in everything, you won't have to look for love in anything!

Believe EVERYTHING that is good about you and doubt, resist, and reject ANYTHING that doesn't agree!

Our greatest joys arise out of the ashes of our darkest moments! Where you are is NOT the end; it's just a pit stop to prepare you for the BETTER DAYS ahead!

As I Reflect ...

Chapter 13

When you only have eyes to recognize what you're afraid of, you spend your entire existence avoiding your fears instead of seeing LOVE and LIVING FEARLESSLY.

When you are constantly agonizing over what you don't have your ingratitude attracts more of the same - WHAT YOU DON'T HAVE!

I asked God to open the eyes of my heart so that I may see ALL that is beautiful - even in the ugly; ALL that is good - even in what looks bad; ALL that is whole - even in what looks broken! And He did.

As I Ponder...

Your evolution is locked inside your personal revolution against being like anyone else!

Yes it's YOUR life; and yes, you can do whatever you like, whenever you like, and however like with YOUR life! Now take a moment and really think before you answer - How is being THAT way really working for you?

Who we are within is who we attract into our lives to reflect back to us the truth about how much we've grown up or not!

What Stirs in My Spirit Is ...

It's never about quantity (how much you get)! The truest meaning of any experience is the QUALITY (how good it is)!

Frequently, those who complain the most are the most resistant to change!

Some people are so used to depending on their desperation to live (survive) that they lack the capacity to even hope or try something different that will cause them to thrive!

As I Reflect ...

If you're reading this you've been tagged to transcend! YOU are the exception to the rule - living between never again and never before!

When you live in gratitude for what you have RIGHT NOW, you won't waste precious moments longing for, or being distracted or frustrated by what you don't have. Before you know it those other things just start showing up!

As I Ponder...

The inoculation of pain in your past was not to destroy you but to make you immune to it in your future. We are all WOUNDED HEALERS! Some folks just choose to stay wounded!

When you conform to the norm you live small! Expand your capacity by making some BIG decisions - trusting that every detail is already worked out!

Sometimes we should just stop and GIVE THANKS for things being as well as they are. It really could have been MUCH worse!

What Stirs in My Spirit Is ...

There can be no peaceful co-existence with ego, fear, doubt, ego, laziness, anger, sadness, ego, low self-worth, arrogance, insecurity, and ego! WARRIOR TRAINING IN FULL EFFECT!

EGO is not confidence! Quite frankly, ego is an exaggerated sense of self (rooted in fear) that always leads back to you feeling not good enough, loved enough, or having enough!

If you wouldn't stand in the rain with me when I had to ENDURE the discomfort of not having an umbrella - please remain on the sidelines as I ENJOY the sunshine, the rainbows, and the people who love me unconditionally!

As I Reflect ...

The litmus test for who REALLY loves you is who STILL shows up when you're in your most unlovable, unpopular, hard to recognize state!

Hear ye hear ye - I decree and declare (with love of course) that I release all who want the privilege of connection without the responsibility of relationship!

When you don't know what to do - BE STILL - wait for peace then proceed! Yes, always follow peace!

As I Ponder...

It's so easy for people to help you make MAJOR decisions when it doesn't cost them anything! Real love leaves evidence!

Be careful when others are pushing you to make major decisions with their words. The truest measure of their support is HOW ARE THEY SHOWING UP FOR YOU WHEN YOU NEED THEM MOST?

People who know better and won't DO better should officially get out of the way of everyone else who want to BE BETTER!

What Stirs in My Spirit Is ...

One day, while walking through an upscale neighborhood I was impressed by how green the grass was until I got closer. It was SPRAY PAINTED! Make sure your image is not a figment of people's imagination!

When your best looks like everyone else's worse; - that's the time to ONLY compare yourself to what God has said about you!

Have courage! Take risks! FAIL! No harm! Learn the lesson! Move on without any judgment of self or others! TRY AGAIN! Succeed!

As I Reflect ...

Some people only deserve to stand in the foyer of your life not sit at your kitchen table. When people are not HONORING your space; love them from a distance!

Don't let what you "see" cause you to forfeit what you "know"! Likewise, don't let what you "think you know" cause you to forfeit the greatness God sees in you!

God, when we don't know how - You do. When we don't know when - You do. When we don't know what - You do. When we don't know who - You do; and I AM OKAY WITH THAT!

As I Ponder...

Your wealth is tied to the thing that talks to you even while you're sleeping; that's why it's called a DREAM!

Just because it has always been that way does not mean it has to BE that way forever! Do something different - NOW!

Significance is not measured by how much stuff you have or how much power you think you have; but by how much love you truly get to experience!

What Stirs in My Spirit Is ...

Champions keep going when everyone else decides to quit! That's the only difference between getting there and not getting there.

When people don't choose you it's not because you weren't the best choice; it's because they weren't the best match!

When you get rid of stuff that does not belong to you (especially other people's doubt and unbelief), your blessings can now land on the runway of your life!

As I Reflect ...

Chapter 14

If they don't want you, it is their loss! If that's not working for you anymore, walk away! If you don't have enough money - increase your income! If you're bored, take some risks and have fun! MY POINT: Be intentional with your happiness daily and anyway!

God is ALWAYS in control even when people "think" they are pulling the strings! Rest assured people can only do what God ALLOWS!

A gentle reminder to treat people the way you want to be treated - PERIOD! Why? Because whatever you do and however you do is ALREADY on its way back to you!

As I Ponder...

The moment you begin to listen to the voice of God within and not so much to the voices of men without, your life will quite suddenly change exponentially for the better!

Sometimes you look back over your life with gratitude and realize the delays were so that God could increase the blessing to fit where you were going - not where you were!

Comforted to know that if God leads you to it, the plan is ALREADY in place to get you through it!

What Stirs in My Spirit Is ...

IT IS WELL, IT IS WELL with my soul; and with yours too! Follow peace today.

Regardless of what is going on in your current context, I assure you that when it's all said and done YOU ARE OKAY! BREATHE!

Live DAILY in the "wonder" of your options; not in the "worry" of lack that may be lingering around! Declare today, that forevermore, you ONLY attract abundance!

As I Reflect ...

Simply put: just because you CAN doesn't always mean you SHOULD!

WHAT IF it doesn't work has kept a lot of people stuck in misery. Likewise, WHAT IF it does work has set a lot of people free.

There is nothing like the power of true friendship! It travels through the good, the bad, the ugly, and the sad.

As I Ponder...

If we invested as much time, money, focus, and mandates on showing love the other 364 days of the year as we do on Valentine's Day, I honestly believe we'd all have stronger relationships! I love you today and every day.

When you stop evaluating, opinionating, and judging how other people should live their lives, you'll have more than enough time to live and love YOUR best life!

At the end of the day, all that really matters are the people who loved you through the easy and the difficult days; and the people whose lives you made better by your journey here!

What Stirs in My Spirit Is ...

Look for miracles in the most unlikely places; coming through the most unlikely people! Please slow down and PAY ATTENTION! You may be next in line for that miracle.

Stop blaming others for what's happening in YOUR life. The gift of insight here is that it's "never" about them; it's all about how that pain helps YOU to grow!

As I Reflect ...

Beloved your house can't hug you, your car won't visit you when you're sick, your job is only good for as long as you meet your employer's needs, and your education is just information. At the end of the day – you must TREAT PEOPLE RIGHT!

I wholeheartedly believe that from this moment forward, I am a magnet for wealth, divine health, wisdom, loving relationships, and uncommon favor! I really do believe that and therefore, these are the ONLY things that will thrive in every area of my life!

So if what keeps showing up in your life IS NOT what you really "want," explore what you "really" believe you deserve!

As I Ponder...

Please know that there are people in your space "solely" to soak up YOUR shine. Give them some light and then send them on their way with love to work on their own life!

Through the lens of compassion, I see countless mean-spirited, not-so-nice, unhealthy, ungrateful, judgmental, and complaining people; and I wonder what it must be like to live with them. Miserable I'm sure. You must be loving and kind to yourself first in order to be truly happy with your life!

If you judge others it follows that you judge yourself! If you are critical of others it follows that you are critical of yourself! Likewise, if you love others unconditionally, it also follows, that you LOVE YOURSELF unconditionally as well!

What Stirs in My Spirit Is ...

Please leave ALL limiting beliefs in yesterday!

The reality of harvest is that no matter how much a farmer desires an abundant crop, NOTHING will happen until the farmer starts planting seeds! This truth applies to ANY area of your life where you desire increase! What are you planting?

Many people hold on tightly to what they have (money, love, etc) in hopes of preserving for later. However, the Principle of Increase is that the more you GIVE AWAY/SOW/INVEST the greater your harvest!

As I Reflect ...

The moment you BELIEVE in your heart that you are a reflection of the essence of God; you begin to attract people in your life who prayed for YOU to show up!

Love people; but don't allow your care for others to make them a priority when you are just an option for them! One of my mentors tells me all the time LOVE UNATTACHED!

Ladies and Gentlemen: everything and everybody cannot go with you into your place of destiny so the "temporary" and "awkward" blindness, loneliness, and discomfort of darkness comes for you to lose the dead weight!

As I Ponder...

The glory of the spotlight comes only after patiently enduring being developed in dark places! You are being broken down to breakthrough to your blessing!

When people want you to change to fit their frame of who you should be, separate yourself ASAP; and BE who God made you to be!

Declare what you desire and then INTENTIONALLY walk in it; "like you already have it," and until you SEE WHAT YOU SAID! This Ladies and Gentlemen is called FAITH!

What Stirs in My Spirit Is ...

When you BE-come all that God made you to BE, then all that BE-longs to you with your name on it LONGS for you and comes looking for you! It's called BE-ing overtaken by your blessings!

The favor of God on my life handles my enemies for me while I enjoy the blessings of the Lord that have ALREADY made me rich without sorrow! GOD IS FAITHFUL!

God illuminated something for me - fear often provokes people to "flee" a situation when it really comes to provoke you to raise your "FIGHT" energy to the next level! FEAR IS FUEL - that's it.

As I Reflect ...

Chapter 15

God will take what seems like nothing at all and make it something MAJORLY wonderful! It's not over yet!

Transparency ALWAYS – always - always leads to transformation! Tell the truth and shame your shame!

If people require you to perform, conform, or deform for their time, love, respect, and attention - TRANSFORM quickly - disappear from their space!

As I Ponder...

Where you are now is not necessarily forever. SNAP OUT OF IT and make one better choice at a time.

Your participation is requested in the manifestation of your next miracle! All you gotta do is BELIEVE that it is on the way and then WAIT WITH GRATITUDE!

If no one told you today, I will, I LOVE YOU!

What Stirs in My Spirit Is ...

It's extremely silly to be "important" with an exaggerated sense of entitlement, especially when people don't know who you are! BE KIND TO EVERYONE!

So grateful for all the things I wanted REALLY badly and God said "ABSOLUTELY NOT!" Whew! THANK YOU GOD!

Often the truth (even when spoken in love) will make you bleed before it makes you BETTER!

As I Reflect ...

Even when you can't see God moving, just know He is working it out in YOUR favor!

Authenticity plus humility plus Integrity equals REAL prosperity!

Live your life so that YOU are happy! I promise it will help other people do the same.

As I Ponder...

Ladies live in your QUEENLINESS and it will create the atmosphere for the men around you to live in their KINGLINESS!

Regardless of what has happened or what "they" did - you get to CHOOSE how you respond. Never let 'em see you sweat! Trust me; the energy is better spent winning in spite of "them"!

Spiritual abuse has the same level of control, codependency, manipulation and cockiness as domestic violence; resulting in WORSE chaos for the recipient! GET TO KNOW GOD FOR YOURSELF! He just does not love like that.

What Stirs in My Spirit Is ...

Healthy personal RELATE-tionships require reciprocity! If you are not bringing anything to the table then you are selfish and can fully expect to get your feelings hurt! If you want something - then BRING something!

If you want to win but don't really EXPECT to win, you're just WISHING!

Truth is most of the lives you impact you will NEVER personally know about! So be your authentic, best self ALL THE TIME. People are watching and they either really want to be like you or they really don't!

As I Reflect ...

Stop making destiny decisions based on the "mean" times you may be currently experiencing! Today's WHAT IS becomes tomorrow's WHAT WAS!

It's very easy to sit back and say what you would do if you were in someone else's shoes. Thing is - you're NOT so if you have nothing loving or encouraging to say ... well you know the rest!

Here is a loving and gentle reminder that God has a way of turning a meaningless moment into a meaningful blessing!

As I Ponder...

Sometimes the best response to adversity, challenges, and obstacles is simply WOW - Wait On Wisdom - for the next move!

Sometimes you don't need to start over, just start from where you are with a renewed perspective and a strong determination not to quit!

I just thought of something: EVERY single day is the eve of a new year! Think how different your life would be if you lived planning the next 365 days this way!

What Stirs in My Spirit Is ...

Afterward

...and before you go, I wanted to share one more thing with my readers. I am blessed to have some very intelligent, spiritually conscious and aware relationships with some remarkable people. I asked one of those friends who I've known for almost 25 years to describe me...

It is not often that people are invited to share unabridged thoughts about someone they know unless the request is motivated by a condition or circumstance. In many instances, depending on the solacing influence of the moment, the descriptive characterizations or jovial expressions merely become solemn utterances or meaningless verbalism. Today I would like to suggest that the manifestation of these thoughts at this moment are in fact a real vista of Vikki and what make me "tick" about her.

When people are young and full of life - ambition, a sense of purpose and the "me" perspective aura attract people to one another. It is at this time of youthful attraction and enlightenment that fraternizing comradeships, unintentional bonds and coquetry affairs are conceptualized. What I saw in Vikki at that time was her fresh and raw beauty, her love for God, her modest disposition, her alluring charm and quest to achieve life's purpose. This may appear on the surface to describe the general population of young adults - "pressing their way" - but when I took the time to survey beneath the veneer of her enchanting persona....what I found is a Gem on a journey, an authentic lady on a path to finding herself and discovering who she "really" is.

In the process of becoming a "grown-up" we all move through life's perils, pitfalls and snares, and we eventually evolve...its nature's way. We either adapt or we become overwhelmed and consumed. After re-connecting and exchanging caring affirmations, Vikki has reminded me of those things I saw when we first met long ago.

For a luminary like Vikki, the pain and effect of life's sometimes destructive and disruptive "growing-up" cycles has proven that if you hold on - GOOD will prevail. Her life has reinforced that as we surrender to life's evolution, new testimonies of God's power, God's grace God's mercy, the strength of LOVE, the power of passion, the addiction of adoration toward oneself and the deity and divines of a Goddess-ness - her very own Vikki-isms if you will. All of this is something that I know about Vikki and it makes me "tick"!

"Rambeau," Author/Blogger of Rambeau's Musings, Renaissance Man & Lifestyle Expert

I hope my words, my life, and my compassion for others makes YOU tick as well! I only want you to squeeze every ounce of self-love from every day because as you do that - then and only then can you give it away.

I'm giving myself away - in the form of Vikki-isms so that even long after I have transitioned from this life to the next, you will have encountered at least one person on the planet who sees nothing but the God in you!

BOOKING INFORMATION/OTHER WORKS

Every Woman Enterprises/Elder Vikki Johnson Ministries
Post Office Box 152
Mount Rainier, MD 20712
301.776.6449
vhkjohnson@yahoo.com
Like Vikki on Facebook: Elder Vikki Johnson
www.vikkijohnson.com

OTHER BOOKS BY VIKKI JOHNSON

Gems For The Journey
More Gems For The Journey
Addicted To Counterfeit Love

CPSIA information can be obtained
at www.ICGtesting.com
Printed in the USA
FSHW020240040719
59639FS